OPTIMISTIC MINDSET

Change Your Thinking,

Build Stronger Relationships,

Enhance   Well-being and Resilience,

and Transform Your Life.

DR. ARUN KUMAAR KHANDA
https://arunkumarrk.com

Copyright © 2024 by Dr. Arun Kumaar Khanda, PhD

All rights reserved.

YOUR FREE GIFT

As a token of my gratitude for taking out time
to read my book, I would like to offer you a
free gift. Click the below link or scan the
 QR code to download your free eBook PDF
https//arun-
kumarkhanda.ck.page/00c46de54c

Acknowledgments

In my journey as an author, I have been blessed with support that has significantly contributed to my success. I am deeply grateful to my mentor and bestselling author, Mr. Som Bathla, for his mentorship, motivation, and guidance in writing, self-publishing, and launching my books, which has been crucial on my path to becoming an author-entrepreneur.

I also extend my heartfelt thanks to my author community, especially to Sooraj Achar, a bestselling author himself, for his timely technical support, encouragement, and invaluable advice, which have made my work much easier.

My gratitude goes out to my readers for their unwavering support. I am also thankful for this incredible platform that provides authors with the resources needed to transform the lives of millions.

Thank you all for being a part of this journey. Readers can connect with me at akkhanda9@gmail.com.

Sincerely,

Arun Kumaar Khanda

MY BEST-SELLING BOOKS

AWAKENING THE SOUL SERIES

1. The Path to God Consciousness

2. **Di**vine Threads: Unravelling the Origins of Religious Beliefs

3. Maya Unveiled: Journey from Illusion to Reality

4. A Journey to Self-Discovery

SUCCESS AND TRANSFORMATION SERIES

1. Crush Your Goals

2. Growth Mindset Blueprint

3. Conquer Your Limiting Beliefs

4. The Art of Selective Attention

5. The Art of Anger Management

6. Unlock the Power of Positive Thinking.

TABLE OF CONTENTS

Preface

Welcome to **"Optimistic Mindset"**! In a world often filled with challenges and uncertainties, maintaining a positive outlook can feel like an uphill battle. Yet, it's precisely in these moments that optimism becomes most valuable. This book is dedicated to exploring the power of optimism and how it can transform your life, relationships, and even the broader world around you.

"Optimistic Mindset" is not just about looking at life through rose-colored glasses. It's about developing a realistic, hopeful perspective that empowers you to navigate difficulties, set and achieve meaningful goals, and foster deeper connections with others. It's about harnessing the incredible strength that lies within a positive outlook and using it to create a life filled with resilience, happiness, and success.

Through this book, you'll discover practical strategies to challenge negative thinking patterns and replace them with empowering thoughts. You'll learn how to build habits that reinforce optimism, even in the face of adversity. We'll delve into the science behind optimism, uncovering how it affects your brain and body, and why it is a crucial component of well-being and mental health.

Moreover, we'll explore how to spread optimism beyond yourself. From creating a supportive network of uplifting people to driving social change, you'll see how your positive mindset can ripple outwards, touching lives and making the world a better place.

With real-life examples and actionable tips, "Optimistic Mindset" aims to provide you with the tools you need to cultivate a brighter, more hopeful outlook. Whether you're looking to enhance your personal life, build stronger relationships, or contribute to a more optimistic society, this book is your guide to embracing and spreading positivity.

Thank you for embarking on this journey with us. May this book inspire you to see the possibilities, embrace challenges with grace, and create a positive ripple effect in your own life and beyond.

Happy reading!

5 Key Takeaways

Chapter 1: What is Optimism and Why Does it Matter?

1. Optimism is Essential for Achievement:

Optimism is more than just positive thinking; it's the driving force behind our actions and success. With an optimistic mindset, we are more likely to set and achieve our goals, handle challenges, and stay motivated.

2. Optimism Impacts Our Brain and Body Positively:

Optimistic thoughts trigger the release of "feel-good" chemicals like dopamine and serotonin in our brains, which promote happiness and motivation. In contrast, pessimism increases stress hormones, leading to anxiety and health issues.

3. Optimism Leads to Better Well-being:

Optimistic people tend to experience more happiness, lower stress levels, and better physical health. This positive mindset helps boost the immune system and contributes to a longer, healthier life.

4. Optimism Enhances Relationships:

When we approach others with kindness, empathy, and a hopeful outlook, we build stronger and more supportive relationships. Optimism can repair and strengthen our connections with others, essential for emotional health.

5. Optimism is About Facing Challenges with Hope:

Optimism doesn't mean ignoring difficulties. It's about acknowledging them, finding solutions, and maintaining hope for a better future. An optimistic mindset helps us overcome tough times with resilience and a positive outlook.

Chapter 2: The Optimist's Advantage

1. Optimism Fuels Goal Achievement:

Optimism provides the energy, motivation, and resilience needed to stay committed to your goals. Optimists focus on solutions and see setbacks as opportunities to learn and grow. They believe in their potential and that of others, which helps them find creative ways to overcome obstacles and stay proactive in their pursuits.

2. Goal Setting is Essential:

Setting clear, specific, and achievable goals (SMART goals) turns dreams into actionable plans. Breaking big goals into smaller, manageable steps makes the journey less overwhelming and keeps you motivated. Effective goal setting involves staying flexible, celebrating milestones, and continuously adapting to changes along the way.

3. Optimism Enhances Relationships:

Optimism improves communication, empathy, and conflict resolution in relationships. By approaching conversations with an open mind and focusing on positive experiences, you build trust and strengthen bonds. Showing appreciation, practicing positive communication, and supporting each other's growth are practical ways to cultivate optimism in your relationships.

4. Optimism Boosts Happiness and Reduces Stress:

Optimists focus on the good in their lives, which enhances their overall happiness. They are more resilient, bounce back quickly from setbacks, and maintain healthier relationships. Their proactive coping strategies and healthier lifestyle choices help reduce stress, leading to lower cortisol levels and better physical and mental well-being.

5. The Ripple Effect of Optimism:

Your optimistic outlook not only benefits you but also influences those around you. By maintaining a positive mindset and clear goals, you inspire others and create a supportive, motivating environment. This ripple effect can lead to a more positive and fulfilling life for both you and your community.

Chapter 3: Challenging Negative Thinking Patterns

1. Understand and Recognize Cognitive Distortions:

Our minds can sometimes play tricks on us, leading to negative thinking patterns called COGNITIVE DISTORTIONS. These are biased ways of thinking that twist our perception of reality, making us feel worse about ourselves and our situations. By identifying these distortions, like all-or-nothing thinking or overgeneralization, we can start to challenge and change them.

2. Challenge and Reframe Negative Thoughts:

When you catch yourself thinking negatively, take a moment to question those thoughts. Are they really true? Look for evidence that contradicts them and try to see the situation from a more positive or balanced perspective. Reframing your thoughts can help you turn challenges into opportunities and feel more optimistic.

3. Practice Gratitude Daily:

Gratitude has a powerful impact on our mental and emotional health. By regularly acknowledging and appreciating the good things in your life, no matter how small, you can boost your happiness and reduce stress. Keep a gratitude journal, thank the people around you, and reflect on positive experiences to cultivate a grateful mindset.

4. Be Kind to Yourself:

We all make mistakes and have imperfections. Instead of being overly critical, practice self-compassion. Treat yourself with the same kindness and understanding you would offer a friend. Recognize that everyone has flaws and that making mistakes is part of being human.

5. Create a Positive Mindset:

Developing a positive outlook can enhance your overall well-being. By focusing on the positives, practicing gratitude, and reframing negative thoughts, you can reduce stress, improve your relationships, and build resilience. Remember, the way you choose to see things can make all the difference, so try to see the world through a more optimistic lens.

Chapter 4: Building Habits for Optimism

1. Adopt a Growth Mindset:

Have a belief in yourself that you can develop your abilities through hard work and learning. This mindset helps you see challenges as opportunities rather than obstacles, leading to better academic, professional, and personal success.

2. Practice Positive Self-Talk:

Encourage yourself with kind and supportive thoughts. Replace negative thoughts with positive affirmations to boost your confidence, reduce stress, and improve your overall mental health.

3. Harness the Power of Visualization:

Use visualization to mentally rehearse your goals. Create detailed, vivid images of success in your mind to prepare your brain and body for real-life achievements. This technique boosts confidence and enhances performance.

4. Combine Visualization with Optimism:

Pair your visualizations with a positive outlook to maximize their effectiveness. Believe that good things will happen, and visualize yourself achieving your goals to build resilience and stay motivated even in tough times.

5. Persevere Through Setbacks:

Understand that setbacks are part of the learning process. Use them as stepping stones toward success, learn from your mistakes, and keep pushing forward with a positive mindset. This resilience is key to achieving long-term success.

Chapter 5: Maintaining Optimism in Difficult Times

1. Acknowledge and Learn from Setbacks:

It's natural to feel upset when things don't go as planned. Take up these feelings and see setbacks as learning opportunities. Ask yourself what you can learn from each experience to grow stronger.

2. Maintain Positivity and Take Action:

Staying positive doesn't mean ignoring the negatives but focusing on possibilities and hope. Surround yourself with supportive people and take proactive steps to address challenges. Remember, optimism is powerful when paired with action.

3. Build Resilience:

Resilience isn't something you're born with—it's a skill you can develop. Strengthen your resilience by fostering positive relationships, staying optimistic, honing problem-solving skills, managing your emotions, and believing in your abilities. Real-life examples, like those of Steve Jobs and JK Rowling, show how resilience can lead to success.

4. Practice Self-Care:

Self-care is crucial for well-being. It reduces stress, improves mood, and boosts physical health. Engage in regular exercise, eat nutritious foods, practice mindfulness, set boundaries, and connect with loved ones. Taking care of yourself isn't selfish—it's essential for maintaining balance and health.

5. Sustainable Optimism Through Self-Care:

Consistent self-care helps build sustainable optimism. When you take care of yourself, you have the energy and clarity to face life's challenges with a positive mindset. Regular self-care practices ensure you stay resilient and maintain a positive outlook over the long term.

Chapter 6: Spreading Optimism: Creating a Positive Ripple Effect

1. Positivity is Contagious and Uplifting

By being positive and encouraging, you can inspire others to see the bright side of life. Simple acts like offering words of encouragement, sharing uplifting stories, and focusing on solutions can significantly impact those around you.

2. Build a Strong Support System

Surround yourself with people who uplift and motivate you. Seek out positive influences and like-minded individuals, nurture meaningful relationships, and avoid toxic connections. A positive support system boosts your mood, reduces stress, and enhances resilience.

3. Optimism Fuels Social Change

Believing in the possibility of a better future can inspire you and others to take action. Whether it's through volunteering, supporting positive initiatives, or encouraging collaboration, optimism drives efforts that lead to meaningful social change.

4. Celebrate Progress and Small Wins

Acknowledge and celebrate even the smallest achievements. This keeps morale high and maintains momentum. Celebrating progress reinforces the belief that positive change is possible and motivates continued efforts.

5. Real-Life Examples of Optimism in Action

Stories of individuals like Elon Musk, Oprah Winfrey, Malala Yousafzai, Sundar Pichai, and Greta Thunberg illustrate how optimism, combined with determination and action, can lead to extraordinary accomplishments and inspire others to make a positive impact in the world.

"Beliefs have the power to create and the power to destroy. Human beings have the awesome ability to take any experience of their lives and create a meaning that disempowers them or one that can literally save their lives." - Tony Robbins

Chapter 1:

What is Optimism and Why Does it Matter?

We are proud to be humans and the most intelligent on this planet. Have you ever thought why you have been made such by the universe, nature, or God (whatever you think fits according to your belief system?) Have you ever asked yourself, why you are superior and unique to other animals? If we remove the prefix word social before animal what would remain? The answer is very specific -animal. Humans and animals share four common factors: *"Āhāra."*/ foods, *Nidra*/sleep, *Bhaya*/fear, and *maithuna*/ sex. But what made you unique to the beast? The answers may be many but the essence is conscience, thinking patterns, resilience, optimism, emotional intelligence, and many more.

Defining Optimism:

"Optimism is the faith that leads to achievement. Nothing can be done without hope and confidence." - Helen Keller

Optimism is a powerful mindset, that has the potential to overcome any challenging situations. It gives the powerless a power boost and the hopeless to hope for a better future. It injects life into the lifeless. You may not proceed a step ahead without an optimistic mindset. Whatever action we are doing every day whether in public or private lives i.e., our job or business or family life all are directly linked with optimism. For example, we perform best in our job to get more salary or appreciation or both. We behave properly to live in peace and let others live in peace. Every step is connected with optimism but it is normally not visible in our daily lives, because we have made it our habit. But when we face challenges in our lives the booster dose of optimism is needed to run the vehicle forward.

What do we need to fulfill our prescribed duties and desires? Here duties and desires may clash with each other, because all the desires may not be included in our duties. Similarly, duties and desires may be individual and community-specific. For example, in poor and middle-class family contexts desires for more money are not considered good, rather the children of such families have been taught to be happy at minimum earnings. However, in rich families, the concept of earning has been reversed. Poor and middle-class people do their duties to meet the minimum expenditures and never step outside their comfort zone. But the rich never fear to face challenges and come out of their comfort zone frequently. In the case of riches, they are very much optimistic about their actions and end result. They continue and upgrade their talent and mental ecosystem to achieve more. Unfortunately, poor and middle-class people never try to upgrade themselves to achieve more, rather pressed under the negativity and often engage in the blame game.

It is a fact that if you are not optimistic about your future, job, career, love, business, or money, nothing can help you or you mayn't be in a race to achieve anything. If you are not optimistic you may not be able to set your SMART goals. You may face problems in decision-making. Can you imagine a life without any goal? It is no less than the life of a beast. Take the example of a street dog, is he able to make his own decision and fix a goal for his future? The answer is known to everyone. Then why are you lagging in choosing a goal? What are the possible reasons? Lack of motivation, laziness, lack of self-love, fear of failure, and more. If you analyze sincerely, you can find the root of all the reasons is one and that is a lack of optimism.

Let me tell you about a recent event. I accidentally met a talented young engineer in a remorseful and frustrated condition a few days back in a restaurant. During the discussion, I learned that he was disappointed due to his breakup with a girlfriend he loved much. Now he conceived the notion that love is bad and girls are not faithful. Then what made him conclude that all girls are unfaithful and cheaters? How cheating of a girlfriend can be attributed to all the girls? What do you think about it?

The answer is not a girlfriend. It is his imagination and pessimism driven by ego. Where ego takes the front seat, he loses his optimistic outlook. Nothing good can happen unless you get rid of your ego-centric emotions. In the case of the young man, his ego made a wall between his thinking pattern and intelligence. Therefore, he is stopped there without taking any actions to come out of the negative emotion. If once the clouds cover the sun, do you believe it is a permanent event or a temporary phenomenon? Every challenge we face in our lives is temporary on this planet.

Change is the law of nature. Be hopeful, be optimistic. Every challenge has a solution.

Remember Buddha says- **"What you think, you become"**.

Optimism is a ray of hope for a better tomorrow, a better future, and a better life.

The Science Behind Optimism:

You are the creator of your own fortune, destiny, and life. You may not blame anybody for your setbacks. Your thinking pattern and thought process can make you happy or put you in stress, and sadness. You are your own best friend when your mind vibrates in optimism and behaves as a foe when it lives in pessimism.

Optimism and pessimism are not only two opposite words, but their impacts are also quite different. Both are associated with two different activities of neurotransmitters in the brain. **Pessimism is associated with the release of a stress hormone called cortisol. Chronically high levels of CORTISOL can increase blood pressure levels, weaken the immune system, and increase stress and anxiety in most cases. On the other**

hand, optimism gives rise to the production of DOPAMINE **and** SEROTONIN NEUROTRANSMITTERS, **promoting happiness, reward, and motivation.** Both hormones are often referred to as "FEEL-GOOD" chemicals because they play a major role in mood, pleasure, and reward.

Dopamine is associated with motivation, reward, and reinforcement. It creates a feeling of pleasure and satisfaction when we complete a task, achieve a goal, or experience something we enjoy such as sex or eating delicious foods. Dopamine also plays a role in movement, learning, and memory. **Dopamine** gives us the desire to take action to earn the exciting rewards that waiting for us. Dopamine is more about the anticipation of reward or pleasure. For example, the feeling you get when you see a delicious meal in front of you or when you get a lovely message from your girlfriend.

Serotonin gives us the feelings of happiness, well-being, and contentment. It also helps regulate sleep, appetite, digestion, and learning. Serotonin is more about feelings of overall satisfaction contributing to a general sense of well-being and calmness. When you are calm, you enjoy peace of mind and heart, giving rise to inner peace and stability in health.

Anxieties, depression, negative thoughts, lack of fulfillment, etc are the causes of health hazards and failure of the immune system. PESSIMISM CREATES BLOCKAGES AND CONFUSION IN YOUR MIND MAKING YOU UNAWARE OF YOUR TRUE ESSENCE AND YOU HAVE THE PATH MISSED. Have you read that drowning people may not get the much-needed lift to escape the scarcity unless the help is restored immediately? But optimism can't lose sight of his goals even if faced with numerous difficulties.

Optimistic thinking can change how our brain works. Research shows that positive thoughts and experiences can make the brain areas responsible for reward, motivation, and emotional control stronger. Being optimistic is also connected to better physical and mental health. It can help boost our immune system and increase the production of hormones that improve our mood.

The Benefits of Optimism:

Optimism is a belief in mind and heart that good things will happen to you or me even if faced with difficulties. It is the strong belief system that may be banking with universal laws and spirituality. It is a mindset that is very close to our hearts and emotions, making a significant impact on our well-being and success.

When we are optimistic our hearts are filled with gratitude leading to more positive emotions. Let me give you a real-life example. In an examination, some questions find their place outside of the syllabus, an average but optimistic student without being worried tries to attempt the questions, but a brilliant but pessimist student attracts negative emotions and leaves the questions unattended. Later the examination board declares grace marks for the out-of-course syllabus questions who have attempted to answer. The result was that the brilliant student could not get the desired result, whereas the optimistic stood first in his institution. The optimism led the average student to take action flooded with positivity without overthinking. Such a type of emotional resilience was found missing in the case of the brilliant. The challenge faced in the exam was a temporary phenomenon for the optimist, who exhibited his resilience at this difficult time.

As an optimist, you are more likely to feel happiness, joy, and contentment often. These emotions not only enrich your mental ability to see the world through a more positive focus and have tangible benefits on physical health. It may lower stress levels, strengthen the functions of the immune system, and even longer life span. Because optimistic people are more vibrated with positive thoughts and actions to keep themselves active and not averse to seeking social support when needed.

Optimism creates a cycle of positivity, producing positive emotions for long-term gain, and keeping us high even during the days of setbacks and adversity. **Further, optimism is not only about positive thinking or, remaining in happy mode it is also about having confidence in a bright tomorrow**. Unlike a fixed mindset, an optimist mindset tries to create a better situation instead of getting stuck on what went wrong. They have the clarity in mind **that "everything shall pass away and time is a great leveler."** They believe in gratitude and are happy with the things they have. They appreciate the things they have without talking about scarcity. The law of attraction doesn't understand positive or negative things or emotions. You attract what you think and remember, it may be positive or negative. When you really analyze and count your blessings, you will be happy to appreciate the blessings of God. Only an optimist can see the bright future swimming through troubled water.

Optimism can repair and restore our broken relationship. When we expect positive outcomes, we behave more politely and approach others with kindness, empathy, and understanding. Such types of approaches can lead to stronger and more supportive relationships, which are essential for emotional health.

However, optimism is not about ignoring the potential setbacks or pretending that everything is right. It is about admitting the difficulties, finding ways to get out of the problem, and maintaining hope for a better future.

Optimism is a source of increased success. When we believe in our own abilities, are likely to set more ambitious goals and start working toward them with determination and resilience. Our positive approach and proactive attitude often give us better performances and greater achievements in different spectrums of life including career, education, health, relationships, research, personal ambitions, etc.

In conclusion, optimism is a mindset that believes in the positive aspects of life. It not only admits the setbacks in life but also tries to find solutions for a better tomorrow with resilience and a positive outlook. Optimism is a source of happiness, success, and greater understanding, that creates positive vibrations in and around us.

Chapter 2:
The Optimist's Advantage.

Optimism and Goal Setting:

The Power of Optimism

Optimism is a source of more energy, self-motivation, and empowerment. It inspires the optimist to take timely action and remain resilient despite difficulties and setbacks. Research has shown that optimists are more likely to stay in their mission of goal setting and working toward its achievement. Because they focus on finding solutions rather than dwelling on problems. **Verywell Mind** points out that

"People with optimistic attitudes are more likely to continue working toward their goals, even in the face of obstacles, challenges, and setbacks. Such persistence ultimately means that they are more likely to accomplish their goals." Further Optimists tend to believe in their own potential and that of others, allowing them to find alternative approaches to difficulties instead of getting discouraged.

They are proactive in their approach toward life and action-takers. Such an approach can lead to more opportunities and a bigger sense of achievement.

The Role of Goal Setting

"Goals are like magnets. They have a way of attracting the things you need to accomplish them." - Mary Kay Ash

Everybody has a dream in his life to achieve. When the dream takes its concrete shape, it becomes the goal. Goal setting is a powerful tool for turning your aspirations into actionable plans. It is about what you want to achieve and preparing a road map to get there. Effective goals are specific, measurable, attainable, relevant, and time-bound, often remembered by the acronym SMART. Big goals are broken down into smaller steps to help you stay focused and motivated throughout your journey.

How Optimism and Goal Setting Work Together

When optimism and goal setting are combined, they create wonder and can propel you toward success. However, your actionable steps with proper planning are important in achieving your goals. Let me explain how:

1. Enhance Motivation: Optimists are naturally more motivated because they believe in the possibility of success. When goals are set with an optimistic mindset, you're more likely to stay committed and enthusiastic, even when faced with challenges.

2. Resilience in the Face of Adversity: Goals are packed with objectives and rarely come without obstacles. Remember obstacles are part and parcel of our journey to destinations. When you find all your roads to success are closed, and no option is left, optimism helps you bounce back from setbacks open a new path, and maintain your focus on the end goal. Instead of getting discouraged by failures, you see them as learning opportunities and a silver lining on the way to success.

3. Positive Reinforcement: Celebrating smaller achievements on the way act as incremental goals. It can boost your confidence and reinforce your optimistic outlook. This positive reinforcement creates a cycle of continuous improvement and success.

"Victory is won not in miles but in inches. Win a little now, hold your ground, and later, win a little more." - Ralph Waldo Emerson

This quote highlights the importance of small steps in a big journey. It reminds us that small drops of water create an ocean. You can't think of flying in the sky without taking a start from the ground.

4. Creative Problem-Solving: Optimists are more likely to think outside the box and find innovative solutions to problems. When they approach goal setting with a positive outlook, they're more open to new ideas and strategies that can help them overcome obstacles. They never think about problems but focus on solutions. It is well-established that the entire universe works on the law of attraction. What you think you become.

Pessimists often encounter problems on the way to accomplishment. Because they often doubted their own abilities and did not find clarity in their actionable steps. When there is no clarity on your actionable steps and systematic planning you may not get the desired results. In contrast, optimistic mindsets are very positive and clear about their road map and future actions.

Practical Steps to Cultivate Optimism and Set Effective Goals

Practice Gratitude:

Start each day by acknowledging things you're grateful for. You may ask why. Because this simple practice can shift your focus from what's wrong to what's right, leading to a more optimistic outlook. It can shift your scarcity mindset to an abundance mindset, making mystery a solution.

<u>Visualize Success:</u>

Spend time imagining what achieving your goals looks and feels like. It is a detailed process of sequences. Visualize it daily for at least half an hour giving emotions of being achieved.

"I visualize this thing that you want, see it, feel it, believe in it. Make your mental blueprint, and begin to build." - William Arthur Ward

Visualization can reinforce your belief in your ability to succeed and keep you motivated.

<u>Set Clear Goals:</u>

Set SMART goals. SMART stands for specific, measurable, attainable, relevant, and time-bound. For example, instead of saying, "I want to get fit," set a goal like, "I will run three times a week for 30 minutes each time on Sunday, Tuesday, and Friday."

<u>Break Down Goals:</u>

Large goals can be overwhelming. Break them down into smaller, manageable tasks. This makes it easier to track your progress and stay motivated.

Stay Flexible:

Be prepared to adjust your goals as needed. Life is unpredictable, and sometimes goals need to be modified. Staying flexible allows you to adapt without losing sight of your overall objective.

Celebrate Milestones:

Acknowledge and celebrate your progress along the way. Recognizing your achievements, no matter how small, can boost your optimism and keep you motivated.

The Ripple Effect of Optimism and Goal Setting

Have you ever thrown a pebble into a tank or pond? If yes you might have observed the smaller waves or ripples traveling all around the tank originating from a single point, where the pebble was dropped. This is called the ripple effect often observed in cases of optimism and goal setting.

Optimism and goal setting not only help you achieve personal success; but also impact those around you. When you approach life with a positive outlook and clear goals, you inspire others and become a role model. Your friends, family, and colleagues are likely to notice your enthusiasm and determination, which can create a supportive and motivating environment for everyone.

Conclusion

Optimism and goal setting are powerful allies on your journey to success. By maintaining a positive outlook and setting clear, achievable goals, you can overcome challenges with resilience and grit. This dynamic duo not only enhances your personal growth but also inspires the people around you. So, start today with a positive mindset and a clear plan, and watch as you achieve more than you ever thought possible.

Optimism and Relationships:

We can't survive without forming good relationships. It is the very foundation of our existence and survival on this planet. We are social because of our relationships nothing less. Fabrication of social bonding is based on the foundation of our relationships. It is part of our fulfillment often overlooked is optimism. Optimism can greatly influence the quality of our relationships, and help us to build stronger, more meaningful connections with others.

Let us explore how a positive outlook can transform your interactions and strengthen your bonds with those around you.

The Power of Optimism in Relationships

"The best and most beautiful things in the world cannot be seen or even heard — they must be felt with the heart." - Helen Keller

For the existence of human beings on this earth, relationship plays very crucial roles. Without a relationship, we are no more humans. However, due to so many reasons, the very fabrics of personal bonding began to shake. During such a critical moment, optimism keeps us alive, hoping for a better tomorrow and better relationships. This way of thinking can really improve your relationships. It helps create a supportive, strong, and fun environment for everyone around you. When upset repeat **"Everything shall pass away. It is a temporary event."** I have practiced it and got the result. It is not just combinations of a few words but its effects on our subconscious mind are impactful.

1. <u>Improve Communication</u>

"Strong relationships are built on mutual respect, trust, understanding, and forgiveness. But most importantly, communication." — Unknown

Optimists tend to communicate more effectively. When you have a positive outlook, you're more likely to approach conversations with an open mind and a willingness to understand the other person's perspective. This leads to more constructive and meaningful dialogues, where both parties feel heard and respected.

For instance, instead of reacting defensively during a disagreement, an optimist might seek to understand the root cause of the issue and work toward a solution. This approach not only resolves conflicts more amicably but also strengthens the relationship over time.

2. Increase Empathy and Support

Optimistic people are generally more empathetic. They can see the good in others and are more inclined to offer support and encouragement. This empathy helps in building trust and a deeper emotional connection.

When your friend or partner is having a hard time, your optimism can give them the hope and comfort they need. Just being there with a positive attitude can really help them deal with their problems better.

3. Better Conflict Resolution

"Conflict is inevitable, but combat is optional." - Max Lucado

All relationships encounter conflicts, but how you handle them can make or break the bond. Optimism plays a crucial role in conflict resolution. An optimistic approach encourages you to see conflicts as opportunities for growth rather than threats.

When you focus on finding solutions instead of dwelling on problems, you're more likely to find common ground and work things out in a way that benefits everyone. This not only fixes the current issue but also strengthens your relationship over time by showing respect and teamwork.

Practical Ways to Cultivate Optimism in Relationships

1. Practice Positive Communication

Start to practice positive communication. This means expressing your thoughts and feelings constructively, avoiding blame, and focusing on solutions. Use "I" statements to communicate your needs without making the other person feel attacked or disrespected.

For example, instead of saying, **"You never listen to me,"** try saying, **"I feel unheard when we don't talk about my concerns."** This shift in language can attract a more open and positive dialogue.

2. Show Appreciation and Gratitude

Use to express appreciation and gratitude regularly can have a profound impact on your relationships. Acknowledge the positive aspects of your interactions and the efforts your partner or friend makes. This not only boosts their mood but also reinforces positive behavior.

Can you imagine the power of **"thank you."**? How much does it impact on relationship and its lasting impression? It is amazing if you feel it in your heart. A simple **"thank you"** or a compliment can go a long way in making the other person feel valued and happy. These two words of appreciation can strengthen your connection.

3. Focus on Positive Experiences

"It is not the differences that divide us. It is our inability to recognize, accept, and celebrate those differences." - Wayne Dyer

It is no doubt that it is difficult to focus on the good moments you have spent together, during unhappy situations. But control your negative emotions and you will find the sign of positivity. Take some time to focus on the good moments and happy memories both shared. Think back on those special moments and plan activities you both love. This can help build a strong foundation of positive feelings that will support your relationship during tougher moments.

4. Encourage Growth and Development

Support each other's personal growth and development. Encourage your partner or friend to pursue their goals and dreams, and celebrate their successes. This can create a sense of partnership and mutual respect.

5. Stay Resilient Together

It is needless to say life is full of ups and downs. Facing these challenges together can strengthen your bond. Maintaining an optimistic outlook can help you both stay resilient. Approach difficulties as a team, supporting each other and finding solutions together. Research says **"Optimists are more likely to see challenges as temporary setbacks... which can help couples maintain a more positive outlook even during difficult times."** (The Power of Optimism in Relationships - Psychology Today psychologytoday.com)

The Ripple Effect of Optimism in Relationships

Optimism doesn't just benefit your direct interactions; it also creates a positive ripple effect. When you approach relationships with a positive mindset, you set a powerful example for others. Your friends, family, and even colleagues are likely to be inspired by your attitude, leading to a more positive and supportive environment overall.

Conclusion

Optimism helps build better relationships. Stay positive and communicate well. Show appreciation and support each other's growth. This creates stronger connections. Embrace optimism and see your relationships thrive. You'll find more joy and satisfaction in your life. This positive outlook can have a profound impact on relationships, as shown by research and expert opinions.

Optimism and Well-being:

In today's fast-changing world, stress and anxiety are common challenges we face. Daily responsibilities and work pressures can take a toll on our mental and physical health. However, optimism, a powerful tool, can help us manage these challenges more effectively. Accepting an optimistic outlook can significantly boost happiness and reduce stress, leading to a healthier and more fulfilling life.

The Connection Between Optimism and Happiness

"The happiest people don't have the best of everything – they just make the best of everything." - Unknown

Happiness is a state of well-being characterized by feelings of joy, satisfaction, and contentment. It is a matter of inner self-fulfillment. It can't be found in the outside world. Optimism plays a crucial role in enhancing happiness for several reasons:

<u>Positive Perspective:</u>

Optimistic individuals focus on what is going right in their lives rather than dwelling on problems. This positive perspective helps them appreciate the good things and enjoy everyday moments. It is about appreciating the things that already have, without running after the mirage. When you realize that God has given you enough to cherish, then you will appreciate the present moment. Definitely, prefer the haves to haven't.

<u>Resilience:</u>

Optimism fosters resilience, the ability to bounce back from setbacks. When optimistic people encounter obstacles, they view them as temporary phenomena. This approach to life reduces the emotional impact of stress and promotes quicker recovery.

<u>Healthy Relationships:</u>

Optimistic people often prefer to have better social relationships. They believe everyone is the gift of one God. All are the same at the energy level. They leave their ego at bay and come forward to make friends. Their positive outlook makes them more approachable strengthening their social support networks. Strong relationships are a key component of happiness.

"There is no happiness like that of being loved by your fellow creatures, and feeling that your presence is an addition to their comfort." - Jane Austen

<u>Goal Achievement:</u>

Optimism keeps us motivated and persistent. When we believe our efforts will pay off, we're more likely to set and reach meaningful goals. This not only boosts our sense of achievement but also makes us feel more satisfied with our progress.

Optimism and Stress Reduction

"The optimist sees the opportunity in every difficulty." - Winston Churchill

Stress is a natural response to challenging situations, but chronic stress can have serious health consequences. Optimism can help reduce stress in several ways:

<u>Stress Appraisal:</u>

Optimistic individuals tend to view stressful situations as challenges rather than threats. This mindset reduces the anxiety associated with stress and allows for the development of more effective problem-solving skills. Optimism can take complicated situations as easy and stop overthinking. But optimism is not about ignoring the risk potential of admitting negative feedback and ignoring important warning signs. Balancing optimism with a realistic understanding of challenges is crucial to avoid setbacks and maintain progress.

<u>Coping Strategies:</u>

Optimists tend to handle stress better because they use proactive coping strategies. They look for solutions, ask others for help, and plan ahead. This positive approach is more effective in managing stress compared to avoidance or denial. By tackling problems head-on and preparing for future challenges, optimists can reduce their stress levels and feel more in control of their situations.

<u>Healthier Lifestyle Choices:</u>

Health is wealth. Our physical body has an unwritten agreement with our mental ecosystem. Stress can destroy both the physical and mental health ecosystem. A healthy lifestyle can give a check to the stress mechanism. Optimistic people are more likely to adopt healthy behaviors, such as regular exercise, balanced nutrition, and adequate sleep. These behaviors help reduce the physical and emotional impacts of stress.

<u>Lower Cortisol Levels:</u>

Research indicates that optimists tend to have lower levels of CORTISOL, which is the hormone our bodies release when we're stressed. Lower cortisol levels mean that optimists experience fewer of the negative physical effects associated with stress. This can lead to better overall health and a greater sense of well-being. By maintaining a positive outlook, optimists are not only better at handling stressful situations but also protecting their bodies from the harmful impacts of stress. Their ability to manage stress more effectively contributes to healthier, happier lives, showing just how powerful a positive mindset can be.

Conclusion

Optimism is a powerful tool for enhancing happiness and reducing stress. By focusing on the positive aspects of life and believing in our ability to overcome challenges, we can improve our well-being and lead more fulfilling lives. However, cultivating optimism is not an easy task. It takes regular practice to make it a habit. I can assure you that start small and turn it into a good habit and see the magic. Your happiness and resilience will definitely grow with the increase of time.

Optimism is not just a feel-good emotion; it's a practical approach to life that can enhance your well-being in profound ways. By consciously adopting an optimistic mindset, you can overcome life's challenges with greater ease and enjoy a happier, more stress-free existence. **Remember, optimism is a skill you can develop and strengthen over time, leading to lasting positive changes in your life.**

Chapter 3:

Challenging Negative Thinking Patterns

Identifying Cognitive Distortions:

"A single bad experience does not define a lifetime. Avoid overgeneralization." - Unknown

Today, let's talk about something that affects all of us at some point: cognitive distortions. These are the sneaky traps our minds set for us, leading to negative thinking patterns that can really bring us down. Understanding these distortions is the first step to overcoming them. So, let's take a look at them together.

What Are Cognitive Distortions?

Cognitive distortions are biased ways of thinking that twist our perception of reality. **David**

Burns, author of the book Feeling Good: The New Mood Therapy, says, **"Cognitive distortions are just tricks our minds play on us."** They often show up as negative thoughts about ourselves, others, and the world. Psychologists have identified several common types of cognitive distortions, each with its own way of distorting our thinking.

Common Types of Cognitive Distortions

<u>All-or-nothing thinking:</u>

This is when we view things in extremes, seeing only black and white. If something isn't perfect, we consider it a complete failure. There's no middle ground or room for mistakes. This all-or-nothing thinking can be really tough because it doesn't allow us to appreciate the progress we've made or the good aspects of a situation. Instead, it makes us focus only on what went wrong, leading to unnecessary stress and disappointment. Seeing the grey areas and **acknowledging that imperfections are part of life** can help us feel more balanced and less pressured.

For example, **if you get a B on a test, you might think, "I'm a complete failure," instead of recognizing that a B is still a good grade.**

<u>Overgeneralization:</u>

This happens when we draw a sweeping conclusion from just one event. Imagine you apply for a job for the first time and don't get it. Instead of seeing it as just one failure or setback, you might think, **"I'll never get a job," "What it will make an impact on my dad," "What my neighbor will think about my talent,"** etc. as if this one rejection means you'll always fail.

This kind of thinking ignores all the other opportunities out there and can make you feel hopeless. It's important to **remember that one event doesn't determine your entire future**. Each experience is just a part of the journey, and other chances will come. Staying positive and open to new possibilities can help you move forward.

<u>Mental Filter:</u>

This is when we zero in on the negative aspects of a situation and overlook the positive ones. For example, imagine in a presentation you receive 10 compliments and one piece of criticism. Instead of enjoying the compliments, you fixate on the criticism, letting it overshadow all the good feedback. This tendency can make you feel unnecessarily upset and undervalued. Recognizing this habit and learning to let go of the negatives is important. Focusing on the positives and keeping a balanced perspective can help you feel more content and confident. Remember, **one critical comment doesn't cancel out all the praise you receive**. Sometimes zealous creates a situation to traps you in destabilization. Remember all the reality and focus your positivity without putting you on negative emotions.

<u>Discounting the Positive:</u>

Similar to the mental filter, this distortion happens when we dismiss positive experiences by convincing ourselves they **"don't count."** For instance, if someone compliments your work, you might think, **"They're just being nice,"** **instead of accepting and appreciating the praise.**

This mindset prevents us from enjoying positive feedback and can undermine our self-esteem. **It's like having a shield that blocks out good experiences, making it harder to feel confident and happy**. Learning to accept compliments and positive feedback can help us build a healthier, more balanced view of ourselves and our achievements. Remember, when someone praises you, they often genuinely mean it, so let yourself believe it and feel good about it.

<u>Jumping to Conclusions:</u>

There are two subtypes here:

- *Mind Reading:* Mind Reading is when you assume you know what others are thinking without any real evidence. For example, if someone doesn't reply to your text, you might immediately think, **"She must hate me."** This kind of thinking can create unnecessary anxiety and misunderstandings. Instead of jumping to conclusions, it's better to communicate openly and give people the benefit of the doubt.

- *Fortune Telling:*

"Your future is created by what you do today, not tomorrow." - Robert Kiyosaki

Fortune Telling is when you negatively predict your future. For example, you might think, **"I'm going to mess up this presentation,"** even though you have no evidence to support it. This kind of thinking can increase anxiety and lower your confidence. Instead, try to focus on preparing well and remind yourself that you can handle the situation.

<u>Magnification and Minimization:</u>

Blowing things out of proportion (catastrophizing) is when you make a minor issue seem like a major disaster. For example, you might make a small mistake at work and think it's a huge failure. Conversely, **"downplaying the importance of positive things"** means you minimize your successes and see them as insignificant. You might achieve something great but brush it off as no big deal. Both of these habits can harm your self-esteem and increase stress. It's important to keep things in perspective and recognize both your challenges and your accomplishments fairly.

<u>Emotional Reasoning:</u>

"You don't see the world as it is, you see it as you are." - R. D. Laing (Scottish psychiatrist)

Emotional Reasoning is when you believe that your feelings reflect reality. For instance, if you feel useless, you might think, **"I feel useless, so I must be useless."** This type of thinking can be misleading because our emotions aren't always based on facts. Just because you feel a certain way doesn't mean it's true. It's important to question these feelings and look at the actual evidence. Remember, EMOTIONS ARE TEMPORARY AND CAN BE INFLUENCED BY MANY FACTORS, so they don't always paint an accurate picture of who you are or what you're capable of.

<u>Should Statement:</u>

It is about setting unrealistic expectations using words like "should," "must," or "ought to." For example, saying **"I should always be happy"** sets a high standard that can lead to disappointment when it's not met. These statements create unnecessary pressure and can make you feel guilty or inadequate when you don't live up to them. It's important to RECOGNIZE THAT LIFE IS FULL OF UPS AND DOWNS, and it's okay not to meet every ideal all the time. Being kinder to yourself and setting more realistic expectations can help reduce stress and improve your well-being.

<u>Labeling and Mislabeling:</u>

Labeling and Mislabeling involves attaching overly negative labels to yourself or others based on actions or situations. For instance, instead of acknowledging a mistake with **"I made a mistake,"** you might harshly label yourself as **"I'm a loser."** This kind of thinking oversimplifies complex situations and can be damaging to self-esteem. It's important to avoid labeling yourself or others in such extreme terms. Instead, RECOGNIZE THAT EVERYONE MAKES MISTAKES and that these do not define your entire identity. Using more constructive language can help maintain a healthier perspective and improve how you feel about yourself and others.

<u>Personalization:</u>

Personalization is a mistake some people make in their lives. I feel is a byproduct of accepting defeat without offering a fight. How can you blame yourself for events outside of your control? If a project fails, you might think, **"It's all my fault,"** even when others were involved. Stop such thinking. Don't blame yourself and hurt your self-esteem. Remember, your self-esteem is your soul of existence and compass in troubled water.

The Impact of Cognitive Distortions

Cognitive distortions are irrational, biased ways of thinking that can significantly impact our mental health. They often lead to negative thoughts about ourselves, others, and our experiences. Common distortions include all-or-nothing thinking, overgeneralization, and catastrophizing.

These distorted thinking patterns can fuel anxiety, depression, and stress. For instance, believing that a single mistake makes you a total failure can lead to feelings of hopelessness and low self-esteem. Research shows that cognitive distortions are linked to various mental health issues. According to a study published in the **"Journal of Behavior Therapy and Experimental Psychiatry"**, INDIVIDUALS WHO FREQUENTLY EXPERIENCE COGNITIVE

DISTORTIONS ARE MORE LIKELY TO SUFFER FROM ANXIETY AND DEPRESSION.

Recognizing and challenging these distortions is crucial for improving mental well-being. By adopting a more balanced perspective, we can reduce negative emotions and enhance our overall quality of life.

How to Combat Cognitive Distortions

The good news is that we can learn to recognize and challenge these distortions. Here are some steps to help:

- <u>Awareness:</u> The first step is to become aware of your negative thoughts and identify the distortions. Find out the situation, event, or person that triggers the negative thinking.
- <u>Challenge Your Thoughts:</u> Ask yourself if your thought is realistic. Look for evidence against it. Are you jumping to conclusions or catastrophizing?
- <u>Reframe Your Thinking:</u> Replace the negative thought with a more balanced one. Instead of **"*I'm a failure*,"** think, **"*I didn't do as well as I wanted, but I can improve.*"**
- <u>Practice Self-Compassion:</u> Be kind to yourself. Understand that everyone makes mistakes and has flaws. No one is perfect on this planet. Imperfection is the trademark of the humans.

Remember Wabi-Sabi (Japanese philosophy) says;

"There is a kind of beauty in imperfection."

SELF-LOVE IS THE KEY TO GETTING OUT OF THE COGNITIVE DISTORTION TRAPS.

Conclusion

Cognitive distortions are common and can significantly affect our well-being, but with practice, we can learn to identify and overcome them. By challenging these negative thinking patterns, we can improve our mental health and lead happier, more balanced lives. Remember the next time you catch yourself in one of these traps, you have the power to change your thinking!

Reframing Negative Thoughts:

Let's talk about something truly reframing negative thoughts. This powerful technique can shift your perspective and bring a brighter outlook to your life. It's all about changing how we think about things to improve our mental ecosystem.

What is Reframing?

"The real difficulty is to overcome how you think about what you are." - Epictetus (Greek Stoic philosopher)

Reframing is a way of looking at a situation, thought, or feeling from a different angle. It's like changing the lens on a camera to get a clearer, more positive picture. Instead of seeing the negatives, you focus on the positives or a more balanced view.

Why is Reframing Important?

Negative thoughts can weigh us down, leading to feelings of stress, anxiety, and depression. RESEARCH SHOWS THAT CONSTANTLY ENGAGING IN NEGATIVE THINKING CAN INCREASE THE RISK OF MENTAL HEALTH ISSUES.

"Once you replace negative thoughts with positive ones, you'll start having positive results." - Willie Nelson (American musician)

Reframing allows you to adjust your perspective and find new ways to interpret the world around you. Imagine you're taking a photograph, and by simply switching the lens, you capture a brighter, more vivid scene. This shift in viewpoint can transform your understanding, turning challenges into opportunities and setbacks into learning experiences. By deliberately choosing to see things in a different light, you can uncover hidden benefits and potential growth in any situation. It's about consciously deciding to look beyond the tinted glass and anticipate a more hopeful and constructive outlook. This ultimately leads to a healthier more optimistic and resilient mindset.

The Science Behind Reframing

Cognitive-behavioral therapy (CBT), a widely used therapeutic approach, heavily relies on reframing. It was developed by Dr. Aaron T. Beck in the 1960s. Studies have shown that CBT can significantly reduce symptoms of depression and anxiety by helping individuals change their thought patterns. For instance, a study published in the **"Journal of Consulting and Clinical Psychology"** found that CBT was effective in reducing anxiety symptoms in 60-80% of patients.

How to Reframe Negative Thoughts

Reframing takes practice, but it's a skill anyone can develop. Make the practice a habit to get its full benefits. Here are some simple steps to get you started:

1. Identify the Negative Thought: Before starting the treatment for a disease, a proper diagnosis is necessary. Treatment follows diagnosis. Pay attention to when you're feeling down or stressed and note what you're thinking. For example, **"I always mess things up,"** and "I

am not capable enough to settle the current issue."

2. Challenge the Thought: Ask yourself if this thought is genuine and accurate. Look for evidence that contradicts it. Have you really always messed things up, or are there times when you've succeeded?

3. Find a Positive Angle: Try to see the situation in a new light. For instance, if you made a mistake, think about what you learned from it. **"I messed up this time, but I've learned something valuable that will help me next time."**

4. Practice Self-Compassion: Treat yourself with kindness. Instead of being your harshest critic, be your own best friend. Remind yourself that everyone makes mistakes and it's part of being human. No one is perfect on this earth. Imperfection is a part and parcel of humanism.

5. Use Affirmations: Replace negative thoughts with positive affirmations. Instead of **"I can't do this,"** say, **"I am capable and can handle this challenge very well."**

Real-Life Examples of Reframing

Here are a few examples of how you can reframe common negative thoughts:

- Negative Thought: "I failed the test; I'm so stupid."

- Reframed Thought: "I didn't do well on this test, but I can study harder and do better next time."

- Negative Thought: "Nobody likes me."

- Reframed Thought: "I have friends and family who care about me. Not everyone has to like me, and that's okay."

- Negative Thought: "I'll never be good at this job."

- Reframed Thought: "I'm still learning and improving every day. Everyone starts somewhere."

The Benefits of Reframing

Reframing can have profound benefits for your mental and emotional health. By shifting your perspective, you can:

➤ <u>Reduce Stress:</u> When you view challenges as opportunities to grow that can lower your stress levels.

➤ <u>Boost Resilience:</u> A positive outlook helps you bounce back from setbacks more easily.

> Enhance Relationships: Positive thinking can improve how you relate to others, fostering better connections.

> Improve Overall Happiness: A brighter outlook leads to greater satisfaction and joy in life.

Conclusion

Reframing negative thoughts is a powerful tool that can change your life. It can shift your perspective, transform challenges into opportunities, reduce stress, and cultivate a more positive, optimistic, and resilient mindset. So next time you catch yourself in a negative thought spiral, take a step back and reframe it. Remember, THE WAY YOU CHOOSE TO SEE THINGS CAN MAKE ALL THE DIFFERENCE. It is upon you how to see the world, through transparent, opaque, or colored glass.

The Power of Gratitude:

Now, let's explore the incredible power of gratitude and how practicing appreciation can bring a positive change into your life. GRATITUDE ISN'T JUST A FEEL-GOOD EMOTION;

IT'S A POWERFUL TOOL FOR ENHANCING MENTAL AND EMOTIONAL HEALTH.

What is Gratitude?

"Gratitude is the fairest blossom which springs from the soul." – Henry Ward Beecher

Gratitude is the act of recognizing and appreciating the good things in your life. It's about acknowledging the positive aspects, no matter how small, and expressing thanks for them. This can be anything from a beautiful sunrise, or a winter evening to a kind word from a friend, or your beloved one.

Why is Gratitude Important?

"Gratitude unlocks the fullness of life. It turns what we have into enough, and more. It turns denial into acceptance, chaos to order, confusion to clarity." – Melody Beattie

Research shows that gratitude has profound effects on our mental health. A study by the University of California, Davis found that people who regularly practice gratitude report higher levels of happiness, optimism, and life satisfaction. They also tend to experience lower levels of stress and depression.

The Science Behind Gratitude

Gratitude impacts the brain in several positive ways. Neuroscientific research indicates that gratitude activates the **brain's reward system**, enhancing feelings of pleasure and motivation. Additionally, it boosts the production of DOPAMINE and SEROTONIN. Both are the **"FEEL-GOOD" NEUROTRANSMITTERS,** which help in reducing anxiety and depression.

A study published in **"Psychological Science"** found that gratitude can even improve physical health. Participants who kept a weekly gratitude journal exercised more regularly, had fewer health complaints, and felt better about their lives overall compared to those who recorded negative or neutral thoughts.

How to Practice Gratitude

Incorporate gratitude into your daily routine in a simple and meaningful way. Here are some simple yet effective ways to practice gratitude:

Keep a Gratitude Journal:

Write down three things you're grateful for each day. They can be big or small. This practice helps you focus on the positives and start your day with a positive mindset. For examples;

> ➢ Thank you, God, for the job I have.

> Thank you, God, for the money I earn.

> Thank you, God, for the food I eat.

> Thank you, God, for the emotional relationship I have.

> Thank you, God, for my good health.

> Thank you, God, for my loving parents.

<u>Express Thanks to Others:</u>

Take time to thank people in your life. Whether it's a quick text, a handwritten note, or a face-to-face conversation. Remember expressing gratitude strengthens relationships spreads positivity and creates mood.

<u>Reflect on Positive Experiences:</u>

At the end of the day, take a moment to reflect on the good things that happened. This can be a peaceful way to wind down and shift your focus away from any stressors.

<u>Practice Mindfulness:</u>

Mindfulness and gratitude go hand in hand. By being present and fully experiencing the moment, you can appreciate the small joys of life more deeply.

<u>Create Visual Reminders:</u>

Place sticky notes or reminders around your home or workspace with things you're grateful for. These visual cues can help keep gratitude at the forefront of your mind.

Real-Life Examples of Gratitude

Here are a few real-life scenarios that illustrate how gratitude can bring a positive shift:

<u>Work Stress</u>: Instead of focusing on the pressures and deadlines, try to appreciate the support from your colleagues and the opportunity to learn and grow in your job.

<u>Family Conflicts:</u> Family dynamics can be challenging, but focusing on the love and care shared within the family can help ease tensions and foster a more harmonious environment.

<u>Daily Hassles:</u> It is a fact that your day is filled with small annoyances. It may be in the form of a traffic jam or a long line at the store. During such hassles, try to find something positive, like

enjoying a favorite song on mobile or having a moment to yourself.

The Benefits of Practicing Gratitude

Practicing gratitude can lead to a multitude of benefits, including:

<u>Improved Mental Health:</u> Regularly practicing gratitude can help reduce symptoms of depression and anxiety, and increase overall happiness.

<u>Stronger Relationships:</u> Expressing gratitude strengthens relationships by fostering a sense of connection and appreciation.

<u>Better Physical Health</u>: Grateful people tend to take better care of their health, exercise more, and have fewer physical complaints.

<u>Enhanced Resilience:</u> Gratitude helps you focus on the positive, making it easier to bounce back from setbacks and challenges.

Conclusion

The power of gratitude lies in its simplicity and profound impact. By practicing appreciation daily, you can experience a significant positive shift in your life. Whether it's through journaling, expressing thanks to others, or reflecting on positive experiences. Integrating gratitude into your routine can enhance your mental, emotional, and physical well-being. So, start today by taking a moment to appreciate the good in your life. God has given you enough material and talent to cherish. A simple and honest mind is needed to appreciate it. Remember, **A GRATEFUL HEART IS A MAGNET FOR MIRACLES**. Miracles may happen at any time, at any moment.

Chapter 4:
Building Habits for Optimism

Developing a Growth Mindset:

Let's talk about something that can truly transform your life. It is about developing a growth mindset. A growth mindset is a powerful approach to thinking that helps you see challenges not as obstacles but as opportunities for growth and learning.

What is a Growth Mindset?

A growth mindset, a concept developed by psychologist Carol Dweck, is the belief that abilities and intelligence can be developed through dedication and hard work. A growth mindset is a belief that skills, intelligence, and abilities can be developed through sincere effort, practice, and learning. The people of growth mindset believe in the philosophy-

"You can change your mind, and you can change your life." - Carol Dweck

This mindset contrasts with a fixed mindset, where people believe their qualities are set in stone and can't change.

The Power of a Growth Mindset

Embracing a growth mindset has profound effects on many areas of life:

> *Academic Achievement:* Studies show that students with a growth mindset achieve higher grades. They view effort as a path to mastery and are more resilient in the face of setbacks.

> *Professional Success:* Employees with a growth mindset are more likely to embrace challenges, persist in the face of adversity, and ultimately achieve higher levels of success.

> *Personal Development:* People who believe in their ability to grow are more likely to set goals, seek feedback, and continuously improve.

The Science Behind Growth Mindset

The idea of a growth mindset is backed by scientific research, especially in two areas: how our brains can change (neuroplasticity) and how our beliefs affect our success.

NEUROPLASTICITY is the brain's amazing ability to change and adapt throughout our lives. Research shows that our experiences can reshape our brains by creating new connections, strengthening existing ones, and improving how fast signals travel between brain cells. This means that with effort and practice, we can improve and learn new skills throughout our lives.

A growth mindset fits perfectly with this. People with a growth mindset believe that intelligence and abilities aren't fixed but can be developed through hard work, learning new strategies, and asking for support. This belief motivates them to tackle challenges, keep going despite setbacks, and see mistakes as chances to learn and improve. Studies have found that students with a growth mindset tend to work harder, get better grades, and have better mental health.

The connection is clear: when we adopt a growth mindset and push ourselves, we exercise our brains, strengthening our neural connections as neuroplasticity suggests. This creates a positive cycle that reinforces the growth mindset and leads to greater success.

In short, the science behind a growth mindset shows that our brains are flexible and capable of significant change. We can use this brainpower to achieve our full potential by accepting a growth mindset.

How to Develop a Growth Mindset

Accept the Challenges:

Challenges create mental stress unless you face them with courage and self-belief. For example, imagine you are walking alone on a country road. You start running seeing a few street dogs. When you are running street dogs can run after you. When you stop and intend to challenge them, they will run away.

"In the middle of every difficulty lies opportunity." - Albert Einstein

See challenges as opportunities to learn and grow. Instead of avoiding difficult tasks, tackle them head-on with the belief that you can improve and can do that.

Learn from Criticism:

It is obvious to be disappointed by criticism. Remember, critics are not your foes but friends. They are the sources of your improvement and further growth. Don't be ashamed to admit the imperfections. It is a stepping stone for improvement. Use feedback as a tool for growth. Constructive criticism helps you identify areas for improvement.

Celebrate Effort:

Focus on the journey and the effort you put in, not just the final result. Understand that hard work and perseverance are essential for growth.

When you focus only on outcomes, it's easy to get discouraged by setbacks or mistakes. But if you appreciate the process and the effort you put in, every challenge becomes an opportunity to learn and improve. This mindset helps you see that success isn't just about talent or intelligence; it's about the determination to keep going, even when things get tough.

Think of it like learning to play an instrument or mastering a sport. It's not just about the final performance or the big game. It's about all the practice sessions, the mistakes you make, and the progress you see over time. Each practice session, each mistake, and each small improvement are all part of your development.

By valuing the effort and the learning process, you build resilience and a stronger foundation for long-term success. You'll find that you can achieve more than you thought possible, simply by staying committed and putting in the work. So, celebrate the small wins, stay persistent, and keep pushing yourself to grow.

<u>Persevere Through Setbacks:</u>

First of all, you have to understand that setbacks are a natural part of learning. Instead of seeing them as reasons to quit, use them as steps toward success.

When we try new things or push ourselves, it's normal to face challenges and make mistakes.

These setbacks aren't failures; they're opportunities to learn and get better. Think of them as part of the journey to achieving your goals. Each time you encounter a difficulty, it's a chance to understand what went wrong, find a solution, and try again.

For example, imagine you're learning to ride a bike. You might fall a few times, but each fall teaches you something new about balance and control. Eventually, those falls lead you to ride confidently. The same idea applies to any skill or goal you're working toward.

It's important to stay positive and keep going, even when things don't go as planned. Remember that everyone faces setbacks, even the most successful people. What sets them apart is their ability to use these challenges as fuel to keep moving forward. They learn from their mistakes, adjust their strategies, and become stronger.

So, when you hit a bump in the road, don't get discouraged. Embrace it as a part of your growth. Keep your focus on the bigger picture and remind yourself that each setback is just another step toward your ultimate success.

Real-Life Examples

Thomas Edison:

He famously failed thousands of times before inventing the light bulb. Edison viewed each failure as a step closer to success. He rightly said **"I have not failed. I've just found 10,000 ways that won't work."**

<u>Michael Jordan:</u>

Michael Jordan is often regarded as one of the greatest basketball players in history. But Jordan was cut from his high school basketball team. He used this setback as motivation to work harder and improve.

Conclusion

Developing a growth mindset can change how you face life's challenges. It helps you see obstacles as chances to grow. Embrace effort, learn from feedback, and keep going even when things get tough. This way, you can reach your full potential and achieve more success. Start today by seeing challenges as opportunities to learn. Never forget, that with a growth mindset, anything is possible!

The Power of Positive Self-Talk:

"Always remember you're braver than you believe, stronger than you seem, smarter than you think, and loved more than you know." - A.A. Milne (author)

Do you know the power of positive self-talk? How does it encourage you? How much does it contribute to your overall success? Positive self-talk is more than just a feel-good concept; it's a practical tool for improving your mental and emotional well-being.

What is Positive Self-Talk?

Positive self-talk means speaking to yourself encouraging, supportive, and optimistic, as you're the best friend. It's about replacing negative thoughts with positive ones, which can boost your confidence and help you tackle challenges more effectively. Remember none other than you can help you better and you are your best friend.

Why is Positive Self-Talk Important?

Research shows that the way we talk to ourselves can significantly impact our mental health and performance.

"Our self-talk matters. It can be our greatest ally or our worst enemy." - Shawn Mendes (singer)

A study published in the **"Journal of Personality and Social Psychology"** found that individuals who engage in positive self-talk are more resilient and better able to cope with stress. Positive self-talk can also enhance performance in areas like sports, academics, and work. When you practice positive self-talk, you're more likely to bounce back from tough times and perform better in various aspects of your life.

The Benefits of Positive Self-Talk

Multifarious benefits you can get from positive self-talk. It can transform your life to a better level sometimes beyond your imagination. Such as;

1. Improve Mental Health: Positive self-talk can reduce symptoms of anxiety and depression. By focusing on the positive, you can create a more optimistic mindset.

2. Enhance Performance: Athletes, students, and professionals who use positive self-talk tend to perform better. Encouraging yourself can increase motivation, focus, and perseverance.

3. Better Stress Management: Positive self-talk helps you manage stress by reframing challenges as opportunities rather than threats. This shift in perspective can reduce the feeling of being overwhelmed and alone during challenging situations.

4. Increased Resilience: When you face setbacks, positive self-talk can help you bounce back more quickly.

"It is during our darkest moments that we must focus to see the light." – Aristotle

It encourages a growth mindset, where you see failures as learning experiences.

How to Practice Positive Self-Talk

It is very easy to practice but you have to be disciplined and regular. Your discipline can turn it into a habit. Your good habits can make you a winner in the struggle.

1. Recognize Negative Thoughts Pattern: Pay attention to your inner dialogue. Notice when you're being overly critical or negative. Which event, situation, or person triggers negative thoughts?

2. Challenge Negative Thoughts: Ask yourself if these thoughts are true or helpful. Often, negative thoughts are exaggerated and not based on reality. Remember your mind plays tricks with you. Challenge the negative thoughts with positive affirmations.

3. Replace with Positive Thoughts: Replace negative thoughts with positive affirmations. Instead of saying**, "I can't do this,"** say, **"I am capable and can handle this challenge."**

4. Be Your Own Cheerleader: Have you seen cheer girls/boys in sports? How they are electrifying the event? Encourage yourself as you would a friend. Use kind and supportive language to boost your confidence. Someone says-

"When in doubt, cheer your heart out." – Unknown

Be your role model and own cheerleader.

Real-Life Examples of Positive Self-Talk

<u>Before a Presentation:</u> Don't come to a conclusion and think negatively. Instead of thinking, **"I'm going to mess this up,"** tell yourself, **"I am well-prepared and I can do this."**

<u>Facing a Difficult Task:</u> Replace **"This is too hard for me"** with **"I can learn and improve with practice."**

<u>After a Setback:</u> Instead of **"I failed,"** think, **"This is a chance to learn and grow."**

Conclusion

The power of positive self-talk lies in its ability to transform your mindset and enhance your overall well-being. By encouraging yourself with positive and supportive thoughts, you can boost your confidence, improve performance, manage stress better, and increase resilience. Start practicing positive self-talk today, and watch how it can lead to greater success and happiness in your life. Remember, you are your biggest cheerleader!

Visualization and Optimism:

You might have heard about a powerful tool such as visualization. It is a fascinating and highly effective technique for boosting confidence. Optimism, coupled with visualization can do wonders in your life and transform how you approach your goals and challenges.

What is Visualization?

"Visualization and belief in a pattern of reality activates the creative power of realization." - A.L. Linall (writer)

Visualization is the process of creating a mental image of a future event. It's like a dress rehearsal in your mind, where you vividly imagine yourself achieving your goals. This technique isn't just about daydreaming; it involves detailed and focused mental practice that prepares you for real-life success.

The Science Behind Visualization

Visualization works by stimulating the same brain regions involved in physical activity. When you vividly imagine performing a task, your brain creates neural pathways that prepare your body to perform the task in reality. This phenomenon is backed by neuroscience.

When you visualize something clearly, your brain interprets it almost as if you're actually doing it. This is because visualization activates the same neural pathways in your brain that are used when you perform the actual activity. So, if you're picturing yourself acing a presentation or winning a race, your brain is already practicing the skills needed to make it happen.

This process helps improve performance and build confidence. Athletes, for example, often use visualization to enhance their physical skills. By mentally rehearsing their moves, they train their muscles and brains together, leading to better performance when they actually compete.

For example, a study published in **"Neuropsychologia"** found that mental rehearsal activates the MOTOR CORTEX, the part of the brain that plans and executes movements. Similarly, research from the **"Journal of Sports Sciences"** shows that athletes who practice visualization improve their performance, sometimes almost as much as those who physically practice.

In summary, visualization leverages the brain's natural processes to prepare you for success. By vividly imagining your goals, you practice and reinforce the skills needed to achieve them, boost your confidence, and stay motivated. It's a simple yet powerful tool that can help turn your dreams into reality.

How Visualization and Optimism Work Together

When you combine visualization with optimism, you create a powerful force for achieving your goals. Visualization lets you picture and practice success in your mind, while optimism gives you the confidence that success is possible. Together, they make you more confident and improve your performance.

Visualization helps you see yourself reaching your goals. When you imagine doing something well, your brain prepares for the actual event by activating the same pathways it would if you were really doing it. This mental rehearsal makes you more skilled and ready when the time comes.

Optimism, on the other hand, is about believing that good things can and will happen. It gives you a positive outlook and the determination to keep going, even when things get tough. When you're optimistic, you're more likely to stay motivated and bounce back from setbacks.

When these two tools are used together, they create a powerful synergy. Visualization shows you the path to success and helps you practice, while optimism gives you the belief and motivation to follow that path. This combination builds your confidence and enhances your performance, making it more likely that you'll achieve your goals. So, by visualizing success and staying optimistic, you set yourself up for great accomplishments.

Steps to Effective Visualization

1. <u>Set Clear Goals:</u> Know exactly what you want to achieve. The more specific your goal, the more effective your visualization will be.

2. <u>Find a Quiet Space:</u> Sit in a quiet place where you won't be disturbed. Close your eyes and take a few deep breaths to relax.

3. <u>Create a Vivid Image:</u> Picture your goal in detail. Imagine the sights, sounds, and feelings associated with achieving it. If you're visualizing a successful presentation, imagine the room, the dais, the color combination of the room, the audience, your voice, and your confident posture.

4. <u>Incorporate All Senses:</u> Use all your senses and paint with emotions to make the image as realistic as possible. The more immersive the experience, the more powerful the effect.

5. <u>Practice Regularly:</u> Like any skill, visualization improves with practice. Spend a few minutes each day visualizing your goals. A specific time slot may be good for the purpose. Make it a habit to get a definite result.

Real-Life Applications of Visualization

Sports:

Many athletes use visualization to enhance their performance. For instance, golfer Jack Nicklaus visualized every shot before playing it. Similarly, Olympian Michael Phelps used visualization to prepare for his races, imagining every stroke and turn.

Public Speaking:

Visualization can help reduce anxiety and build confidence. Before a speech, imagine yourself speaking clearly and confidently, receiving positive feedback from the audience.

Career Success:

Visualizing success in job interviews, presentations, and meetings can improve your performance. Picture yourself answering questions confidently and engaging with colleagues positively.

The Benefits of Combining Visualization and Optimism

1. Increase Confidence: Rehearsing success in your mind builds the belief that you can achieve it. This confidence translates into real-life situations, making you more likely to succeed.

2. Reduced Anxiety: Visualization can help reduce anxiety by familiarizing you with challenging situations. When the actual event occurs, it feels more manageable because you've already "EXPERIENCED" it.

3. Enhanced Performance: By mentally practicing a task, you improve your skills and readiness, leading to better performance.

4. Greater Resilience: Optimism helps you stay motivated and persistent, even in the face of setbacks. Visualizing positive outcomes reinforces this mindset, making you more resilient.

Conclusion

Visualization and optimism are powerful tools that can significantly enhance your confidence and performance. By vividly imagining your success and maintaining a positive outlook, you prepare your mind and body for real-life achievements. Start incorporating these practices into your daily routine, and watch how they transform your approach to challenges and goals. Remember, **THE FIRST STEP TO ACHIEVING ANYTHING IS BELIEVING YOU CAN**—so visualize, stay optimistic, and make your success a reality!

Chapter 5:

Maintaining Optimism in Difficult Times

Coping with Setbacks:

Life is full of ups and downs, and setbacks are a natural part of the journey. While it's easy to get discouraged when things don't go as planned, adopting an optimistic mindset can make all the difference. Here's how you can cope with setbacks, learn from challenges, and bounce back stronger than ever.

Acknowledge the Experience

First and foremost, it's important to acknowledge your feelings. It's okay to feel upset, frustrated, or disappointed when things go wrong. Allow yourself to experience these emotions without judgment. Don't live in it. Remember it as a temporary phenomenon. This acceptance is the first step toward moving forward.

Find the Lesson

Every setback carries a lesson. Instead of seeing challenges as failures, view them as opportunities to learn and grow. Ask yourself:

- "What can I learn from this experience?"

- "How can this make me stronger?"

Reflecting on these questions helps shift your perspective and extract valuable insights from difficult situations.

Stay Positive

Maintaining a positive attitude doesn't mean ignoring the negative aspects of a setback. It's about focusing on the possibilities and remaining hopeful. Surround yourself with supportive people who uplift you, and engage in activities that boost your mood and energy. POSITIVITY FUELS RESILIENCE. Remember the following famous quote;

"The pessimist sees difficulty in every opportunity; the optimist sees the opportunity in every difficulty." - Winston Churchill

Take Action

Optimism is a daydream if not backed by action. Once you've processed your emotions and extracted the lessons, it's time to take action.

Create a plan to address the setback and set small, achievable goals. Taking proactive steps not only helps you regain control but also builds momentum toward overcoming the challenge.

Practice Self-Compassion

Be kind to yourself. Setbacks are a part of life, and everyone experiences them. Avoid self-criticism and instead, practice self-compassion. Treat yourself with the same understanding and encouragement you would offer a friend in a similar situation.

Stay Persistent

Resilience is built through persistence. Keep pushing forward, even when progress feels slow. Remember that setbacks are temporary, and with determination and effort, you can overcome them. Each step you take brings you closer to your goals.

Celebrate Your Progress

Finally, celebrate your progress, no matter how small. Acknowledging your achievements, especially after overcoming a setback, reinforces your resilience and boosts your confidence. It's a reminder of your ability to bounce back and thrive.

In conclusion, coping with setbacks is about embracing the experience, learning from the challenges, and taking positive action to move forward. With an optimistic mindset, you can turn setbacks into stepping stones, and each challenge becomes an opportunity for growth. Keep believing in yourself, and remember that you have the strength to bounce back from any setback life throws your way.

Developing Resilience:

Resilience is the remarkable ability to bounce back from adversity. It's a trait we can all develop. Research shows that resilience isn't something we're born with—it's a skill that can be cultivated through experience and practice. Here's how you can build resilience and strengthen yourself through life's challenges.

Understanding Resilience

Resilience is often described as the capacity to recover quickly from difficulties. Psychologists have found that resilience involves behaviors, thoughts, and actions that can be learned and developed by anyone. It's about-facing adversity with a constructive attitude and the determination to overcome obstacles. We must understand that-

"When we long for life without difficulties, remind us that oaks grow

strong in contrary winds and diamonds are made under pressure." - Peter Marshall

Key Components of Resilience

1. <u>Positive Relationships:</u> Strong connections with family, friends, and community provide support and encouragement during tough times. Research shows that having a reliable support network is crucial for resilience. These relationships offer emotional support, practical help, and a sense of belonging.

2. <u>Optimistic Outlook:</u> Maintaining a hopeful and positive perspective helps you see beyond the immediate difficulties. Studies suggest that optimism is linked to better mental health and greater resilience. Believing in a better future can motivate you to keep going even when the going gets tough.

3. <u>Problem-Solving Skills</u>: Effective problem-solving skills enable you to tackle challenges head-on. Research indicates that resilient individuals are better at finding solutions and making decisions under pressure. Practicing these skills can make you more adaptable and resourceful.

4. <u>Emotional Regulation</u>: Managing your emotions, especially in stressful situations, is a key aspect of resilience. Techniques like mindfulness and cognitive-behavioral strategies help in maintaining emotional balance. Research

supports that emotional regulation is crucial for bouncing back from setbacks.

5. Self-Efficacy: Self-efficacy is a belief in your ability to influence events and outcomes to boost your resilience. Studies show that a strong sense of self-efficacy helps you take on challenges with confidence and persist through difficulties.

"Self-belief does not necessarily ensure success, but self-disbelief assuredly spawns failure." - Albert Bandura (the psychologist who coined the term self-efficacy)

Building Resilience: Practical Steps

1. Cultivate Connections: Nurture your relationships with loved ones and seek out meaningful new social connections. Join groups or communities where you feel valued and supported making you encouraged even in tough times.

2. Foster Optimism: Practice seeing the positive aspects of situations. Keep a gratitude journal, and remind yourself of your strengths and past successes. Never feel disappointed by temporary setbacks. Remember setbacks are there to make you stronger. It is a natural part of human experience.

3. Enhance Problem-Solving Skills: Engage in activities that challenge your problem-solving skills. This could be as simple as puzzles or as complex as taking on new projects at work.

4. Practice Emotional Regulation: It is the emotional ecosystem where we often fail. Incorporate mindfulness practices into your daily routine. Techniques like deep breathing, meditation, and yoga can help you stay calm and focused.

5. Boost Self-Efficacy: Set small, achievable goals to build your confidence. Celebrate your successes and learn from your mistakes.

Resilience in Action: Real-Life Examples

Overcoming Personal Loss:

In most situations losing near and dear is beyond repair and compensation. Individuals who have lost loved ones often find resilience through the support of friends and family, and by finding meaning in their experiences. Writing, painting, music, or any other form of creative expression can be a great way to process their emotions and create something beautiful.

Volunteering time or resources to a cause their loved one cares about can be a way to connect with their memory and make a positive impact in their name.

They may consider starting a foundation or scholarship in their loved one's name if have wealth. This can be a lasting legacy that helps others and keeps their memory alive.

Professional Setbacks:

Entrepreneurs who face business failures often develop resilience by learning from their mistakes and trying again with new strategies. Their determination and adaptability lead to eventual success. Professional setbacks also include job loss. By developing resilience, one can get a better job and opportunities to excel.

For examples,

Steve Jobs: Ousted from Apple in 1985, Jobs co-founded NeXT and Pixar, both of which were highly successful. He eventually returned to Apple in 1996 and led the company to even greater heights.

Oprah Winfrey: Fired from her first television job in Baltimore, Oprah went on to become one of the most successful media moguls of all time.

JK Rowling: Rejected by multiple publishers, Rowling's Harry Potter series went on to become one of the best-selling book series of all time.

Health Challenges:

People dealing with chronic illnesses or serious health conditions often demonstrate resilience. It is in the form of making a treatment plan, maintaining a positive outlook, and seeking support from healthcare professionals and peer groups. We have seen many people recover from the disease like cancer.

For examples,

Manny Pacquiao: Boxing champion Manny Pacquiao revealed in 2016 that he had been diagnosed with stage 4 nasopharyngeal cancer. Underwent treatment and recovered, returning to boxing and even running for the Philippines senate.

Kylie Minogue: Pop icon Kylie Minogue was diagnosed with breast cancer in 2005. She underwent treatment and has since returned to music and acting. She is a strong advocate for early detection of cancer.

Robin Roberts: ABC's Good Morning America anchor was diagnosed with breast cancer in 2007 and myelodysplastic syndrome (MDS) in 2012. She underwent successful treatment for both conditions and continues to be a powerful voice for cancer survivors.

In conclusion, resilience is not an innate trait but a skill that can be developed through intentional practices and supportive relationships. By understanding and cultivating the key components of resilience, you can build strength through adversity and emerge stronger from life's challenges. Remember, resilience is about not just surviving but thriving despite the difficulties you face.

The Importance of Self-Care for Maintaining Your Well-being.

"An empty lantern provides no light. Self-care is the fuel that allows your light to shine brightly." – Alexis Mateo

In our fast-paced world, self-care often takes a backseat to the demands of daily life. However, scientific research consistently highlights the critical role self-care plays in maintaining well-being and for the development of sustainable optimism. Here's a detailed look at why self-care is essential and how it helps you stay positive and resilient.

Understanding Self-Care

Self-care refers to activities and practices that we engage in regularly to reduce stress, maintain emotional intelligence, and enhance our health and well-being. It's about taking deliberate actions to care for our mental, emotional, and physical health. Contrary to the notion that self-care is indulgent or selfish, it's a vital component of a healthy, balanced life.

"Self-care is not selfishness. You cannot pour from an empty cup." – Eleanor Brown

The Science Behind Self-Care

1. Mental Health Benefits:

Stress Reduction: Research shows that self-care practices, such as mindfulness and relaxation techniques, significantly reduce stress levels. Chronic stress can lead to a range of health problems, including anxiety, depression, and cardiovascular issues. Self-care helps mitigate these effects by promoting relaxation and reducing the production of stress hormones like **CORTISOL.**

Improved Mood: Activities that promote self-care, like exercise and hobbies, stimulate the release of **ENDORPHINS** and other neurotransmitters that enhance mood. Studies indicate that regular self-care can decrease symptoms of anxiety and depression, fostering a more positive outlook on life.

2. Physical Health Benefits:

Better Sleep: Good sleep is an important and integral part of self-care. It is linked to improved health issues. Quality sleep supports physical health by boosting the immune system, repairing tissues, and regulating hormones. Research suggests that people who practice self-care routines, including consistent sleep schedules, experience better sleep quality and overall health.

<u>Enhance Immune Function</u>: Regular physical activity is a key component of self-care. It has been shown to strengthen the immune system. EXERCISE INCREASES THE CIRCULATION OF IMMUNE CELLS, HELPING THE BODY FIGHT OFF INFECTIONS MORE EFFECTIVELY.

Our immune system's "warriors" include:

- *Phagocytes*: These cells destroy bacteria and viruses.
- *Neutrophils:* The most common phagocytes, the first to respond to infections.
- *Macrophages:* Versatile phagocytes that also activate other immune cells.
- *Lymphocytes:* B cells produce antibodies; T cells kill infected cells and regulate the immune response.
- *Dendritic cells*: Connect the innate and adaptive immune systems.
- *Natural killer* (NK) cells: Kill infected and tumor cells.
- *Mast cells:* Involved in allergic reactions and inflammation.

Balanced nutrition also supports these cells, helping maintain good health. By working together, these different immune cells can protect us from a wide range of threats. A healthy immune system is essential for maintaining good health and preventing illness. Additionally, balanced nutrition, another self-care aspect, provides essential nutrients that support immune function.

3. Emotional Health Benefits:

<u>Increase Resilience:</u> Self-care practices build emotional resilience by helping individuals manage stress and recover from setbacks more effectively. Engaging in activities that bring joy and relaxation helps maintain emotional balance, making it easier to cope with life's challenges.

<u>Strengthen Relationships:</u> Taking time for self-care can improve relationships by reducing irritability and increasing patience and empathy. When we are well-rested and less stressed, we are more present and engaged in our interactions with others. When you are relaxed you are more optimistic about a healthy relationship. Without a vibrant relationship, we are no less than a beast.

Practical Self-Care Strategies

1. Physical Self-Care:

Exercise Regularly: Aim for at least 30 minutes of moderate exercise most days of the week. Activities like walking, cycling, yoga, and swimming are excellent for both physical and mental health.

Eat Nutritious Foods: Prioritize a balanced diet rich in fruits, vegetables, whole grains, and lean proteins. Proper nutrition supports physical health and enhances mood.

2. Emotional Self-Care:

Practice Mindfulness and Meditation: Spend a few minutes each day practicing mindfulness, breathing exercises, or meditation to reduce stress and improve emotional well-being.

Engage in Hobbies: Make time for activities that you enjoy and that bring you joy, whether it's reading, gardening, painting, or playing an instrument.

3. Mental Self-C care:

Set Boundaries: Learn to say no and set boundaries to protect your time and energy. This helps prevent burnout and ensures you have time for self-care.

<u>Seek Professional Help:</u> If you're struggling with mental health issues, don't hesitate to seek help from a therapist or counselor. Professional support is a crucial component of self-care.

4. Social Self-Care:

<u>Connect with Loved Ones:</u> Spend quality time with friends and family. Strong social connections are vital for emotional health. It provides you strength and moral courage to feel as one among us.

<u>Join Support Groups:</u> Consider joining groups that share your interests or experiences. Support groups provide a sense of community and belonging.

The Link Between Self-Care and Sustainable Optimism

Sustainable optimism is the ability to maintain a positive outlook over the long term, even in the face of challenges. Self-care is foundational to this kind of optimism. When we prioritize self-care, we build a reservoir of physical and emotional strength that helps us stay resilient. By regularly engaging in self-care practices, we ensure that we have the energy and mental clarity to face life's ups and downs with a positive attitude and mindset.

In conclusion, self-care is not a luxury but a necessity for maintaining well-being and promoting sustainable optimism. The scientific evidence is clear: taking time to care for yourself has profound benefits for your mental, emotional, and physical health. By incorporating self-care into your daily routine, you can enhance your resilience, improve your mood, and build a more positive, optimistic outlook on life. Remember, taking care of yourself is the first step toward a healthier, happier you.

Chapter 6:

Spreading Optimism: Creating a Positive Ripple Effect

The Power of Positivity:

Positivity is like a light that can brighten up even the darkest of days. When we encourage optimism in others, we help them see the brighter side of life, no matter what challenges they might be facing. Here's how we can harness the power of positivity to uplift those around us.

1. Be a Role Model

It is not easy to become a role model. But your dedication and optimism can put you on that spot. People often look up to those around them for cues on how to think and act. By staying positive and demonstrating a hopeful outlook, you can inspire others to do the same. Show them how you handle tough situations with grace and optimism. Your attitude can be contagious!

<u>2. Offer Encouragement</u>

Sometimes, most of us need a little encouragement to keep going. Simple words like **"You can do it," "I believe in you,"** or **"You're doing great"** can make a huge difference. When people feel supported, they are more likely to stay positive and push through difficulties.

<u>.3. Share Positive Stories</u>

Stories of success and resilience can be incredibly motivating. Share examples of individuals who overcame obstacles through their positive attitudes. These stories can provide hope and inspire others to believe that they, too, can succeed despite challenges.

<u>4. Focus on Solutions, Not Problems</u>

When faced with difficulties, it's easy to get bogged down by focusing on the negatives. Encourage others to look for solutions instead of dwelling on problems. Help them brainstorm ways to overcome obstacles and remind them that every problem has a potential solution.

5. Practice Gratitude

Gratitude is a powerful tool for fostering positivity. Encourage others to reflect on the good things in their lives, no matter how small. Keeping a gratitude journal or simply taking a moment each day to acknowledge what they are thankful for can shift their focus from what's wrong to what's right.

6. Be a Good Listener

"Listening is a magnetic and strange thing, a creative force. The moment someone truly listens, not only the speaker but the listener is changed." - Muriel Barbery

Sometimes, people just need someone to listen to them. By being a compassionate listener, you can provide emotional support and help others feel understood and valued. This can alleviate their stress and contribute to a more positive outlook.

7. Celebrate Small Wins

Celebrating small achievements can boost morale and keep motivation high. Encourage others to recognize and celebrate their progress, no matter how minor it may seem. Each small victory is a step toward a bigger goal.

8. Stay Connected

Isolation can lead to negative thinking and melancholy. Encourage social connections and foster a sense of community. Whether it's through regular check-ins, group activities, or simply spending time together. Staying connected can provide emotional support and encourage a positive mindset even during challenging situations.

Why It Matters

Encouraging optimism in others doesn't just help them—it also creates a ripple effect that can lead to a more positive environment for everyone. Optimism can improve mental and physical health, increase resilience, and enhance overall well-being. By fostering positivity, we contribute to a happier, healthier, and more supportive community.

Remember, positivity is a powerful emotion. It can create positive vibrations in and around us to motivate others. Motivation ignites optimism in the people which can project the bright side of life and inspire them to achieve their best.

Building a Positive Support System:

Surrounding yourself with uplifting people is like planting a garden with flowers that bloom all year round. The right support system can provide encouragement, boost your mood, and help you thrive in every aspect of your life. Here are a few steps for building a positive support system and why it's so important.

1. Identify Positive Influences

Look for people who radiate positivity and can bring out the best in you. They may be friends, family members, or colleagues who encourage you, celebrate your successes, and support you during tough times. Identify those who make you feel good about yourself and motivated to achieve your goals.

2. Seek Like-Minded Individuals

"Surround yourself with people who make you happy, and who inspire you to become the best version of yourself." – Roy T. Bennett

Join groups or communities that share your interests and values. Whether it's a hobby club, a sports team, or a professional organization. Remember "Birds of a feather flock together." Accompany of like-minded individuals can provide a sense of belonging and mutual support. These connections can be a source of inspiration and encouragement.

3. Nurture Meaningful Relationships

Invest time and energy into nurturing your relationships. Regularly check in with your friends and family, share your experiences, and show genuine interest in their lives. Strong, meaningful relationships are built on mutual trust, respect, and support.

4. Be Selective with Your Time

It's important to spend your time with people who uplift you rather than those who bring you down. Pay attention to how you feel after interacting with different individuals. Be aware of toxic relationships. If someone consistently drains your energy or makes you feel negative, it is better to disconnect them. It is foolish to spend your valuable time with people of a negative perspective. Remember, time is very precious. You may not waste it with unholy partnerships.

5. Offer Support to Others

Being part of a positive support system isn't just about receiving encouragement—it's also about giving it. Be there for your friends and loved ones when they need your support. Offering a listening ear, kind words, or practical help strengthens your relationships and creates a reciprocal cycle of positivity. Believe in giving knowledge and wisdom for other's upliftment. Can you imagine the value of a dazzling and smiling face? Your unwavering support can do wonders for others.

6. Communicate Openly and Honestly

Good communication is key to any supportive relationship. Be open about your needs and feelings, and encourage others to do the same. Honest communication helps build trust and an environment of a positive ecosystem. Let others in your support system understand how to best support each other.

7. Celebrate Together

Celebrate together the successes and milestones of the people in your support system, no matter how big or small. Whether it's a promotion at work, completing a personal project, or even just a good day.   Sharing in each other's joy strengthens your bonds and fosters a positive atmosphere.

Why a Positive Support System Matters

Having a positive support system can significantly impact your mental and emotional well-being. Here's why it matters:

- Boosts Your Mood: Positive, uplifting people can boost your mood and make you feel happier.

- Reduces Stress: Supportive relationships can help you manage stress more effectively. Knowing that you have people to lean on can provide comfort and reduce anxiety

- Increases Motivation: Uplifting people encourage you to pursue your goals and dreams. Their support and encouragement can increase your motivation and drive.

- Enhances Resilience: A strong support system helps you bounce back from setbacks. The encouragement and advice from your network can help you to overcome challenges more effectively.

- Improves Health: Positive social interactions can have a beneficial effect on your physical health. Studies have shown that supportive relationships can boost your immune system and contribute to a longer, healthier life.

Conclusion

Building a positive support system is about surrounding yourself with people who uplift, encourage, and support you. These relationships are like a safety net, providing strength and comfort during tough times and sharing joy during good times. By investing in positive relationships, you create a nurturing environment where you and those around you can have a win-win situation. So, take the time to cultivate your garden of uplifting people—it's one of the best investments you can make in your overall well-being.

Optimism and Social Change: Creating a Brighter Future for All

Optimism is a powerful force that can drive social change and create a brighter future for everyone. When we believe in the possibility of a better world, we are more likely to take action to make it a reality. Here's how optimism can fuel social change and how you can contribute to creating a positive impact.

<u>1. Believing in Possibility</u>

Optimism starts with believing that change is possible. God is there around us. When one door is closed many doors are opened. It's about seeing challenges as opportunities rather than invincible obstacles. When people have a positive outlook, they are more motivated to work toward solutions, no matter how difficult the problem may seem. This belief in possibility is the first step toward making a difference.

2. Inspiring Action

Optimism inspires action. When we are hopeful about the future, we are more likely to take steps to create that future. Whether it's volunteering for a cause, participating in community events, or advocating for policy changes, optimistic individuals are often at the forefront of social movements. Their positive energy can inspire others to join the cause and work together for change.

3. Building Strong Communities

Optimism helps build strong, supportive communities. When people come together with a shared vision of a better future, they create a sense of unity and purpose. This collective optimism can lead to collaborative efforts to address social issues, from improving facilities in local schools to tackling climate change. Strong communities are the backbone of social change, and optimism helps strengthen these bonds.

4. Overcoming Adversity

Optimism helps people overcome adversity. Social change often involves facing significant challenges and setbacks. Optimistic individuals are resilient; they persist in the face of difficulties because they believe in the potential for improvement. This resilience is crucial for sustaining long-term efforts to bring about social change.

<u>5. Spreading Hope</u>

Hope is contagious. When people see others working optimistically toward social change, it inspires them to get involved. This spreading of hope can create a ripple effect, leading to broader participation and greater impact. By maintaining a positive outlook and sharing it with others, we can amplify our efforts and reach more people.

How You Can Foster Optimism and Drive Social Change

1. Educate and Raise Awareness

Educating yourself and others about social issues is a crucial step. Knowledge empowers people to take action. Share information through social media, community events, or informal conversations. Raising awareness helps people understand the importance of the issues and the role they can play in making a difference. It may include social, political, or judicial reforms.

2. Support Positive Initiatives

Get involved in or support initiatives that promote positive change. This can be through volunteering, donating, or simply spreading the word. Supporting organizations and movements that align with your values can amplify their impact and help create a brighter future.

3. Be a Positive Role Model

Lead by example. Show others how optimism and positive actions can lead to meaningful change. Your behavior can inspire others to adopt a similar outlook and get involved in social change efforts.

4. Encourage Collaboration

Social change is more effective when people work together. Encourage collaboration within your community or networks. Bring people together to discuss issues, brainstorm solutions, and take collective action. Collaboration harnesses the strengths and ideas of many, making efforts more impactful.

5. Celebrate Progress

Acknowledge and celebrate the progress made, no matter how small. Celebrating successes keeps the momentum going and reinforces the belief that positive change is possible. It also boosts morale and motivates people to continue their efforts.

Conclusion

Optimism is a vital ingredient for social change. It drives us to believe in the possibility of a better future, inspires action, builds strong communities, helps us overcome adversity, and spreads hope. By fostering optimism in ourselves and others, we can contribute to creating a brighter future for all. Remember, every positive action, no matter how small, contributes to the larger goal of social change. Together, with a positive outlook and a commitment to action, we can make a difference and build a better world.

Realtime Examples

We can find hundreds of real-time examples in our society. Let us meet the individuals and how their optimism has contributed to their success:

Elon Musk

Elon Musk is a visionary entrepreneur known for founding and leading multiple groundbreaking companies, including Tesla, SpaceX, Neuralink, and The Boring Company. His journey has been marked by bold ideas and relentless optimism in the face of adversity.

Tesla: When Musk took over Tesla, the electric vehicle industry was struggling to gain traction. Traditional car manufacturers and many investors were skeptical about the feasibility of electric cars. However, Musk's unwavering belief in a sustainable future powered by clean energy led him to push through financial and technical challenges. Today, Tesla is a leader in the electric vehicle market, setting new standards for innovation and environmental consciousness.

SpaceX: Musk's ambition to revolutionize space travel with SpaceX was initially met with skepticism and several failed rocket launches. Despite these setbacks, Musk remained optimistic about making space travel more affordable and accessible. His perseverance paid off when SpaceX successfully launched and landed reusable rockets, significantly reducing the cost of space missions. The company's achievements include the first private spacecraft to dock with the International Space Station and plans for crewed missions to Mars.

Elon Musk's optimism and determination have not only driven his personal success but have also inspired a new era of innovation in the technology and space industries.

Oprah Winfrey

Oprah Winfrey is a globally recognized media mogul, actress, and philanthropist whose life story is a testament to the power of optimism and resilience. Born into poverty in rural Mississippi and facing numerous personal hardships, Oprah's early life was challenging.

Talk Show Success: Oprah's big break came when she hosted a local talk show in Chicago, which eventually became "The Oprah Winfrey Show." Her authentic and empathetic approach to interviews resonated with audiences, making her show a massive success. Oprah's ability to connect with people on a deep emotional level and her optimistic outlook on life helped her build a media empire.

Philanthropy and Advocacy: Beyond her show, Oprah has used her platform to advocate for various social issues, including education, health, and empowerment for women and children. She established the Oprah Winfrey Leadership Academy for Girls in South Africa, providing education and opportunities to underprivileged girls. Her optimistic belief in the potential for positive change has inspired millions to take action in their communities.

Oprah Winfrey's success story illustrates how optimism, combined with hard work and empathy, can transform lives and create lasting impact.

Malala Yousafzai

Malala Yousafzai is a Pakistani activist for female education and the youngest-ever Nobel Prize laureate. Her story is a powerful example of how optimism and courage can drive significant social change.

Early Advocacy: Growing up in the Swat Valley in Pakistan, Malala became an outspoken advocate for girls' education at a young age. Despite threats from the Taliban, who opposed girls' education, she continued to speak out, blogging for the BBC and appearing in documentaries.

Surviving the Attack: In 2012, Malala survived a gunshot wound to the head in an assassination attempt by the Taliban. Instead of being silenced, the attack strengthened her resolve to fight for education. Her optimism and bravery captured global attention and rallied support for her cause.

Global Impact: After her recovery, Malala co-authored the memoir "I Am Malala" and established the Malala Fund, which advocates for girls' education worldwide. Her efforts have helped increase awareness and funding for educational initiatives in developing countries.

Malala Yousafzai's optimism and resilience in the face of extreme danger have made her a symbol of hope and empowerment for young people everywhere, demonstrating the profound impact one individual can have on the world.

Sundar Pichai

Sundar Pichai, the CEO of Alphabet Inc. and its subsidiary Google LLC, is a shining example of how optimism and perseverance can lead to remarkable success.

Early Life and Education: Growing up in a modest family in India, Pichai exhibited an early interest in technology and engineering. Despite limited resources. His optimism and academic excellence earned him a scholarship to Stanford University, where he pursued his graduate studies in materials science and engineering.

Career at Google: Pichai joined Google in 2004, initially leading product management and innovation efforts for a suite of Google's client software products, including Google Chrome and Chrome OS. His optimistic vision for user-friendly and accessible technology played a crucial role in the success of these products. Chrome, in particular, became the most popular web browser in the world under his leadership.

Leadership and Vision: Pichai's calm, optimistic, and inclusive leadership style earned him respect and trust within Google. He was appointed CEO of Google in 2015 and later of Alphabet Inc. in 2019. Under his leadership, Google has continued to innovate and expand into new areas such as artificial intelligence and cloud computing. His optimistic outlook on the future of technology and its potential to improve lives has driven the company's continued growth and success.

Sundar Pichai's journey from a humble background to leading one of the world's most influential tech companies underscores the power of optimism, education, and hard work.

Greta Thunberg

Greta Thunberg, a Swedish environmental activist, is a powerful example of how optimism and determination can lead to global impact, especially in addressing critical issues like climate change.

Beginning of Activism: Greta began her activism at the age of 15 by striking from school to protest outside the Swedish parliament, calling for stronger action on climate change. Her solo protest quickly gained international attention and inspired millions of students around the world to join her in what became known as "Fridays for Future."

Global Influence: Despite her young age, Greta's optimistic belief that young people can drive significant change has been central to her activism. She has spoken at numerous high-profile events, including the United Nations Climate Change Conference, where her passionate speeches have called on world leaders to take immediate and decisive action to combat climate change.

Continuing Impact: Greta's optimistic and unwavering commitment to her cause has galvanized a global movement. She has been nominated for the Nobel Peace Prize multiple times and continues to inspire activism and awareness about environmental issues across the globe.

Greta Thunberg's story highlights how optimism, especially among youth, can lead to powerful movements and significant progress in addressing global challenges.

These examples, demonstrate that optimism, when combined with determination and action, can lead to extraordinary accomplishments and inspire others to create positive change in the world.

Conclusion

OPTIMISTIC MINDSET has taken you on a journey through the transformative power of optimism. We've experienced what optimism truly is, beyond the simplistic notion of looking at the world through rose-colored glasses. We've acknowledged the science behind it, revealing how a positive outlook can reshape your mind and body, leading to numerous benefits including greater resilience and increased success.

Through understanding the optimist's advantage, you have learned how setting goals with a positive mindset can enhance your achievements, how optimism can strengthen your relationships, and how it can significantly boost your well-being and reduce stress. You've also uncovered the traps of negative thinking and how to challenge and reframe these thoughts to cultivate a brighter perspective. The practice of gratitude has been highlighted as a powerful tool for shifting your mindset toward positivity.

Building habits for optimism involves developing a growth mindset, which sees challenges as opportunities for growth. Positive self-talk and visualization are key techniques for fostering confidence and encouraging yourself toward success. Even in difficult times, maintaining optimism is possible through effective coping strategies, resilience, and self-care, ensuring that your optimism is sustainable.

Finally, we have discussed the ripple effect of spreading optimism. By encouraging positivity in others, building a supportive and uplifting network, and contributing to social change, you can help create a brighter future for everyone.

As you close this book, remember that optimism is not about ignoring life's challenges. It's about facing them with a mindset that is hopeful, resilient, and proactive. By accepting an optimistic mindset, you are choosing to see opportunities where others see obstacles. You are committing to a life of growth, happiness, and success. Carry these lessons with you, and let your optimism shine, not just for yourself but for those around you. Together, we can create a world filled with hope and positivity.

Disclaimer

This book is for educational purposes only. Readers acknowledge that the author does not render legal, financial, medical, or professional advice. The content within this book has been derived from various sources. Please consult a licensed professional before attempting any techniques outlined in this book.

By reading this document, the reader agrees that under no circumstances is the author responsible for any direct or indirect losses incurred as a result of the use of the information contained within this document, including but not limited to errors, omissions, or inaccuracies.

Adherence to all applicable laws and regulations, including international, federal, state, and local governing professional licensing, business practices, advertising, and all other jurisdictions, is the sole responsibility of the purchaser or reader.

Neither the author nor the publisher assumes any responsibility or liability whatsoever on behalf of the purchaser or reader of these materials. Any perceived slight of any individual or organization is purely unintentional.

May I Ask You for a Small Favor?

At the outset, I want to give a big thanks for taking out time to read this book. You could have chosen any other book, but you chose mine, and I totally appreciate this.

I hope you got at least a few actionable insights that will have a positive impact on your day-to-day life.

Can I ask for 30 seconds more of your time?

I would love it if you could leave a review about the book. Reviews may not matter to big-name authors; but they're a tremendous help for authors like me, who don't have many followers. They help me grow my readership by encouraging folks to take a chance on my books.

To put it straight, reviews are the lifeblood of any author. I feel this book **"OPTIMISTIC MINDSET"** shall enrich you with some actionable steps.

Please leave your review by visiting the **"Review Section** "of this book's page on this platform.

It will just take less than a minute of your time, but will tremendously help me to reach out to more people, so please leave your review.

Thanks for your support of my work. And I would love to see your review.